Don't
Be Afraid
to Love

Don't Be Afraid to Love

Poems and notes on love, friendship,
family and women's independence

Susan Polis Schutz

Designed and illustrated by
Stephen Schutz

Blue Mountain Press ™

Boulder, Colorado

Library of Congress Number: 84-71149
ISBN: 0-88396-221-7

Manufactured in the United States of America
First Printing: September, 1984

Blue Mountain Press INC.

P.O. Box 4549, Boulder, Colorado 80306

CONTENTS

Photo by Stephen Schutz

Photo by Barry Staver

INTRODUCTION

This last year has been the best year of my life. I gave
birth to a beautiful baby boy and had a lot of fun with my
other two children. I wrote a book. Stephen and I did many
exciting things while working and playing together every
day. Certainly all these things contributed to my happiness,
but much more important was the underlying love. My love
for Stephen and my family gives me the strength and
confidence to enjoy everything that is beautiful in life and to
fight against all the ugly things in the world. I really do feel
that if people would be honest with themselves and each
other and were not so afraid to love, the world would be a
far better place to live.

In this book, I have included handwritten notes about why
I have written the poems and about my thoughts and
philosophy. I hope that these notes will add some insight
into my life and feelings. Perhaps you might even
understand your own life a little better after reading them.

DON'T BE AFRAID TO LOVE.

Susan Polis Schutz

Everyone has been hurt probably more than once by people whom they love. But you must be willing to forget any bad experiences and open yourself up to the possibility of a new love.

SPS

Don't be afraid
to love someone
totally and completely
Love is the most fulfilling
and beautiful feeling in the world
Don't be afraid that you will
get hurt
or that the other person
won't love you as much
There is a risk in
everything you do
and the rewards
are never so great
as what love can bring
So let yourself get involved
completely and honestly
and enjoy the possibility
that what happens
might be the only real
source of happiness

When I entered college, several friends and I made a list of characteristics that "the man we fall in love with" would have. I was quite serious about the list. The first time I met Stephen I knew that he possessed all the qualities I liked, plus a lot of important ones that I left out.

SPS

In my dreams
I pictured a person
who was
intelligent, good-looking
sensitive, talented
creative, fun
strong and wise
who would completely
overwhelm me
with love
Since dreams
can be just
wishful thinking
I did not really expect
to find one person
who had all these
outstanding qualities
But then —
I met you
and not only did you
bring back my
belief in dreams
but you are even
more wonderful
than my
dreams

I know that
I can share any experience I have
with my few good friends, and
they will understand everything
I am going through. A friend with
whom you can only share the good
times or the bad times is not
really a friend at all.
SPS

You have known me
in good and
bad times
You have seen me
when I was happy
and when I was sad
You have listened to me
when what I said was intelligent
and when I talked nonsense
You have been with me
when we had fun
and when we were miserable
You have watched me
laugh
and cry
You have understood me
when I knew what I was doing
and when I made mistakes
Thank you for
believing in me
for supporting me
and for always being ready
to share thoughts together
You are a perfect friend

When I first decided to open
up to Stephen, I communicated
some of my deepest feelings
via notes and poems.
It does not matter how
you do it, but it is vital
to always be honest with
the person you love.

SPS

When we first met
I held back so much
afraid to show my deepest feelings
As I got to know you better
your gentleness and honesty
encouraged me to open up
and I started a trust
in you that I never had
with anyone else
Once I started to express
my feelings
I realized that
this is the only way
to have a relationship
It is such a
wonderful feeling
to let myself
be completely known to you
Thank you
so much
for showing me
what two people can
share together
I look very forward to
spending many beautiful
times with you

A friend of
mine was complaining
to me about her husband.
Being objective, I told her I
was sure that some things that
she did bothered her husband
tremendously and that
she could not expect
perfection from anyone,
including herself. I
wrote this poem for her.

SPS

Things aren't always
perfect between us
but everything
worth anything
has flaws
in it
No one is perfect
therefore no
relationship can be perfect
Often by seeing
the dry brown petals
in a rose
you appreciate more
the vivid red petals
that are so beautiful
And I do appreciate
our very special relationship
which is so important to me
As we continue
to grow
as individuals
our relationship
will continue to grow
more beautiful
every day

I received a letter from an
old friend, and I meant to
call her every day for two
years, but there was always
something else to do.
Finally I called her, and our
conversation was so rewarding
that I promised myself I
would pay more attention
to my dear friendships.

SPS

There are so many things
to do each day
There is so much going on in the world
of great concern
that often we do not stop and think about
what personally is really important
One of the nicest things in my life
is my friendship with you
and even if we don't have a lot of time
to spend with each other
I want you to always know
how much I appreciate you
and our friendship

It is very difficult
for a woman
to have a
successful career and
happy children and an
exciting personal life

When attending to work
most women feel guilty
because they are not with their children
When attending to their children
most women feel guilty
because they have work to do
And if there is time
for personal things
most women feel guilty
because they are neither
attending to the needs of their children
nor their work

In order for a woman
to successfully do
all the things she wants to
she must delegate the things
she does not want to do —
and her husband must equally
share all the family
responsibilities
Otherwise
all the demands
on the woman
leave her
too tired and frustrated
to enjoy life
And that just isn't fair

It has been said
by people whom I otherwise admire
that, "As long as there
is a family structure,
women will be forever oppressed."
I do not agree with this
In fact, I believe the opposite to be true

A family can give a woman
    the freedom and backing
    to go out in the world
    and become a success
    at whatever she wants to do

A family is a structure built on love
    from which a woman will
    forever have support
A family is a relationship
    that will grow through
    good and bad times
A family is a commitment
    to help each other
    to be as happy as possible in life
A family is a security that one
    might not otherwise have in the
    vast world
A family is thousands of shared experiences
A family is inspirational
A family can give you the needed confidence
    and happiness to achieve great things
    in the aggressive world

A woman must be strong enough
to oppose any type of oppression
Or better yet, she must
be smart enough
to enter a relationship
with someone who is her equal
and will not oppress her
because she is a woman
Only in this way can
a family be all the
things it can so
beautifully be

I wrote this to
a friend who was having
personal problems. She lost confidence
in herself. I tried to remind
her of her outstanding qualities,
and I tried to give her
my fullest support as a
friend.

SPS

I know that lately you
have been having problems
and I just want you to know
that you can rely on me for anything
you might need
But more important
keep in mind at all times
that you are very capable
of dealing with any complications
that life has to offer
So
do whatever you must
feel whatever you must
and keep in mind at all times
that we all
grow wiser and
become more sensitive and
are able to enjoy life more
after we go through
hard times

I look at some couples who seem to have
lost that sparkle in their eyes
and I know that can never happen to us
because we have such a deep and
    meaningful relationship —
one that is exciting and fulfilling in every way
And because I never want us to take
    each other for granted
I want to treat each day as if we were new
    to each other
I know how hard it is to find a relationship like ours
and I thank you every day and every minute
for being such a beautiful part
of my life

So many couples I know,
who used to be extremely
happy together, barely talk
or look at each other now.
I always wonder what made
their relationship change so
dramatically.
    I think most couples,
after a little bit of time, take
each other for granted and
don't work at being loving
partners anymore.
Nothing can stay great
without working at it.
                    SPS

Some people laugh at love
They laugh at marriage
They laugh at happiness

It is because they have had
bad experiences that deeply hurt them
They are cynical now, doubting
anything in life that is beautiful

Don't listen to these people
Love is essential to a happy life
So take risks
Love with all your heart
Love with all your mind
It will be more than worthwhile

A friend told me
that she was getting married
despite her peers laughing
at her. People can be
cruel. When laughing at her,
they were probably wishing that
they had a good relationship
with someone.
You have to be so strong and
rise above people's
criticism of your life
in order to
be happy.
SPS

It is not important that partners
have the same qualities and
characteristics. What is important
is for each person to respect,
love and accept each other
exactly the way they are.

SPS

I often wonder what
made us fall in love
with each other
We are so different
from each other
Our strengths and weaknesses
are so different
Our ways of approaching things
are so different
Our personalities
are so different
Yet our love
continues to grow and grow
Perhaps the differences we have
add to the excitement of our relationship
and I know that both of us as a team
are stronger than either of us alone
We are basically different from
each other
but we have so many
feelings and emotions in common
And it really doesn't matter
why we fell
in love
All that matters to me
is that we continue
to love each other
forever

My three-year-old daughter was going to have her tonsils taken out. She was extremely scared. We took her to the hospital where she would be having the operation. She saw a movie showing how tonsils are removed. She met the anesthesiologist and the surgeon and asked them many questions. She tried on the mask that would put her to sleep. She knew that her throat would hurt after the operation. We all told her as much about it as we could, and she very intelligently said, "I don't really want my tonsils out, but I'm not afraid, because I know I'll feel much better when it's done, and I know you'll be there when I wake up." After she said this, I wrote this poem in honor of her. Children are so wonderful!

SPS

When you interact with children
you must always keep in mind
that everything you do and say to them
has an enormous impact on their lives
If you treat children
with love and respect
it will be easier for them
to love and respect themselves and others
If you treat children
with freedom and honesty
it will be easier for them
to develop confidence in their
abilities to make decisions
If you treat children
with intelligence and sensitivity
it will be easier for them
to understand the world
If you treat children
with happiness, kindness and gentleness
it will be easier for them
to develop into adults capable
of enjoying all the beautiful things
in life

Being a romantic,
I expected marriage to
be a classical love relationship
where the man and woman remain
in a state of ecstatic love. People
always laughed when I told them
that this is what I expected if I got
married. I backed away from a lot
of relationships, turning down
marriage proposals because I
knew that they would not be the kind
of marriage I wanted. When I did get
married, my romantic idea of
marriage came true! If you know
what you want and you pursue
it adamantly, your dreams
can come true.

SPS

When I was younger I dreamed
how marriage should be
a sharing of goals
and lives
a love so strong that
it is always exciting and growing
a blending of two imperfect individuals
into stronger, better people
who laugh more, accomplish more
are happier, more successful, and more at peace
My dream came to be
because you had the same dream as I
and I want you to always know
how thankful I am
for our beautiful marriage
and how much I love
my life with you

My darling daughter
I am so glad that
you were born in an age
when women are so
aware of what is going on
and don't always have
to fight so hard to be heard
The world is wide open
for you to be whatever you want
It will be hard
but at least you
will find other women
striving for the same thing
and you won't be called "crazy"
for wanting to achieve your goals
Though full equality
is a long way off
there certainly have been changes
that will make your life as a woman
not so stereotyped and confined
You are living in an age
where womanhood is
   finally growing
to be everything
that it can be
My darling daughter
I watch you play with
   dolls and trucks
footballs and toads
and I see you
   my beautiful child
in the future
as a beautiful woman
in full control of her life

To My Daughter

Since you were born
you have been
such a beautiful
addition to our family
Now that you are growing up
I can see that
you are a beautiful
addition to the world
and I am so
proud of you
As we watch you
doing things on your own
we know you will find
happiness and success
because we are confident in
your ability
your self-knowledge
your values
But if you ever need a boost
or just someone to talk to
about difficulties that might be occurring
we are always here
to help you
to understand you
to support you
and to love
you

My Son

From the day you
were born
you were
so special
so smart
so sensitive
so good
It was so much fun
    to watch you
As you grew
you became your
own person
with your own
ideas
and your own way
of doing things
It was so exciting
    to watch you
As you grew more
you became more
    independent
still special
still smart
still sensitive
still good
I am so proud
of everything about you
and I want you to know
that I love
everything about you

I have always heard
parents say
"Wait until the terrible twos" or
"Wait until the talkative threes" or
"Wait until the fearsome fours" or
"Wait until the crazy teens"
You never fit these clichés
At every age you have been
so interesting and inquisitive
so beautiful and cute
Every day and every year have been
complete miracles —
a child learning so much
about the world
I have always been so
lucky and proud to be able to
be around you
to enjoy with you
your new-found experiences
and to share your
enormous love
You have always been
nothing but
pure joy and love
in my life
and you always will be
Thank you, my son

I don't like clichés. They are like stereotypes, unscientific and inaccurate. Every person is a complicated individual who does not conform to a few descriptive adjectives.
SPS

To My Mother

It is so nice
to have a grandmother
visit with her grandchildren
There is a very special
bond between the two
Both know that
neither is directly responsible for
the behavior of the other
but yet
the familial tie
is so strong
This results in a
relaxed relationship based on
love and giving into each other completely
Grandmothers play games
with their grandchildren
that parents would never play
Grandmothers take their grandchildren
to places that parents
would not think of
Grandmothers give their grandchildren
an understanding of heritage
that the parents cannot give
Grandmothers and grandchildren
frolic in happiness in each other's presence
I am so glad
that my children
can have this wonderful, unique and
beautiful
relationship
with you

It is so unfortunate that grandparents and grandchildren often live far from one another and they very rarely see each other. One thing we need in the world today is the wisdom, security and love of our elder people, mixed with the innocence, curiosity and energy of our younger people.
SPS

An ideal mother should be
strong and guiding
understanding and giving
An ideal mother should be
honest and forthright
confident and able
An ideal mother should be
relaxed and soft
flexible and tolerant
But most of all
an ideal mother should be a
loving woman
who is always there when needed
and who
by being happy and satisfied
with herself
is able to be happy and loving
with her children
Mom, you are a rare woman —
you are everything an
ideal mother should be

When you have a mother
who cares so much for you
that anything you want
comes before her desires

When you have a mother
who is so understanding that
no matter what is bothering you
she can make you smile

When you have a mother
who is so strong that
no matter what obstacles she faces
she is always confident in front of you

When you have a mother
who actively pursues her goals in life
but includes you in all her goals
you are very lucky indeed

Having a mother like this
makes it easy to grow up
into a loving, strong adult
Thank you for
being this kind
of wonderful
mother

When you return
to the place you were raised
you become closer to the truth

When you walk through the old field
where you used to play
you will see how things have changed

When you see the people you grew up with
and start to talk to them
you will learn that people remain the same

Though places and things disappear
   or change with time
true friendships only grow stronger with time

It is always so comfortable to see you
or hear from you
Thank you for always remaining
one of my
closest friends

I went back to Peekskill, N.Y., my small home town, and visited my old gray house. The stores are all boarded up. The school is no longer there. Our high school hang-out is now a grocery store.

But the trees are the same, the skating pond is still there, and the people are the same. I felt out of place, but very comfortable.

SPS

I think about you so much
I wonder if you are having fun
I wonder if you are happy
I wonder if you are feeling well
Though we don't see each other very often
you are with me all the time
in my thoughts

What can you expect out of
Life? Only what you dream and seek.
Everyone asks me how it feels to
be famous, how it feels to have people
read my work, and they ask me how
did I ever accomplish so much.

The answer is that being well-known for
one's work is extremely fulfilling, and I am
certainly very thankful for this. I worked hard
and had big dreams to follow. But what is
even more important is that I am doing
what I want to do, and I
have found love.

SPS

A woman will get only what she seeks
You must choose your goals carefully
Know what you like
and what you do not like
Be critical about what you can do well
and what you cannot do well
Choose a career or lifestyle that interests you
and work hard to make it a success
Enter a relationship that is worthy of
everything you are physically and mentally capable of
Be honest with people, help them if you can
but don't depend on anyone to make life easy
or happy for you
Only you can do that for yourself
Strive to achieve all that you like
Find happiness in everything you do
Love with your entire being
Make a triumph
of every aspect
of your life

This is the happiest
time of my life
I sit and listen to the waves
break against the rocks
and I watch the white seagulls
dance in and out of the water
I feel the wetness of the air
leave a dew on my cheeks
I appreciate so much the
beauty of unadulterated nature
This is the happiest
time of my life
I sit and talk to you
about everything I think of
and I watch so proudly
all that we have
created together
I feel our love overwhelmingly in
every part of my body and mind
I appreciate so much the
beauty of our pure relationship
I am very lucky indeed

Come with me
to feel the beauty
of the mountains
the serenity of the sea

Come with me
to hear the
roaring of the waves
the crackling of the thunderclouds

Come with me
to see the stars shine
the fading sunset over the hills

Come with me
to express our feelings
to express our love

I got together with some
of my friends with whom
I grew up. We knew each
other's backgrounds and families
so well that, though many
of us hadn't seen each other
for a very long time, we still had
an enormous understanding
of each other.

SPS

We were friends
when we attended school together
Since then
we have followed different paths
living in different places
We grew apart
yet we grew together
Our years of sharing
and discussing
every thought, every idea,
and every experience
led us to know each other
so very well
No new friend could ever understand
us as we understand each other
Though we don't see each other
as often as we used to
our friendship still
grows stronger
every day

Love is beautiful
Love is sharing
Love is the giving and taking between two people
who feel so deeply about one another
Love is sensitive
Love is overwhelming
Love is the most important emotion one can have
But
Love is not always simple
Love is not always uncomplicated
Love may not always be easy
but it is
always more than worthwhile

Believe in yourself
Get to know yourself
what you can do and what you cannot do
for only you can make your
life happy

Believe in work, learning and achieving
as a way of reaching
your goals
and being successful

Believe in creativity
as a means of expressing
your true feelings
and as a way of
being spontaneous

Believe in appreciating life
Be sure to have fun every day
and to enjoy
the beauty in the world

Believe in loving
Love your friends, love your family
love yourself, love your life

Believe in long-term relationships
Be sure the people are worthy of your love
and be very honest with them

Believe in your dreams
and your dreams can become
a reality

Most people say that
with time
relationships are supposed to be
boring and
uninteresting
not exciting and
not fun
But our relationship
with time
is more interesting
more exciting and
more fun
Our relationship is the
most important
part of my life
and I always strive
to keep it this way
and I know that
you do, too
Most people say that
with time
the best aspects of a relationship end
but with time
our relationship
gets better and better
and our love gets
stronger and stronger
Thank you for a
relationship that
disproves what most people say

More than ever
I love you
More than ever
I admire you
More than ever
I like you
More than ever
I respect you
More than ever
I want you
forever

It is not true that love weakens with time. If you and your partner are interested in many things together; are appreciative of the beautiful things in life; are able to spend time on your relationship; and remain exciting people alone and together, your respect and love for each other should grow with time.

SPS

This year
I realized that
my career is just
what I always
dreamed that it might be
My love for my husband
is stronger and more exciting
than ever
My children are
more beautiful and fun
than I ever hoped they could be
This year
I felt it was exactly
the ideal time
to have
another
child

Jorian

You are the
happiest
most content
most loving
baby I have
ever seen
I am so
thrilled to be
your mother
In the short
six months of your life
you have become
so loved and
so much a part
of our family
We are so very thankful
that you are here

October 6: In the delivery room I was
wide awake with Stephen next to
me when my baby boy, Jorian,
was born by a cesarean section.
He was healthy, beautiful and
happy! As Stephen held him,
tears of happiness and relief
flowed uncontrollably from
my eyes onto the
baby's cheeks.
What a miracle!
SPS

Darling Jorian

My perfect little
baby boy
You go to sleep
smiling
You wake up
smiling
Your eyes are
so warm
Your dimples
are so happy
Love radiates
from every
part of you
You are truly
a perfect little
baby boy
whom I will smile with
forever

On the ski slopes
in Colorado
sitting in an outdoor cafe
everyone smiling
talking about the ski conditions
and how the weather is
All problems are forgotten
in this quaint fairyland
There is not a good reason why
this kind of worriless existence
isn't carried over
to the real world

I still love Joan Baez
as I did many years ago
Her voice, so pure and feeling
makes me so emotional
Her causes, so idealistic and true
make me think about all
the injustices in the world
And I'm proud to be part of
a generation that patterned
our lives in the same way
that Joan Baez did because
we all want the same thing —
love, peace and freedom

There are many people
that we meet in our lives
but only a very few
will make a lasting impression
on our minds and hearts
It is these people that we will
think of often
and who will always remain
important to us
as true friends

There are so many
sad and terrible things
in the world —
and often it is impossible
to smile
but when I am with you
I can only
think of all the
happy and good things
in the world
and I feel a constant
smile in my heart
I love
you

Sometimes I look at you
and I need a little more
reassurance that you love me
Even though I know
how much you love me
I would like for you
to tell it to me over and over again
And just in case you feel that way also
I am writing you this
to tell you over and over again
that I love you

My love for you
is present everywhere —
in my career
in my happiness in nature
in my appreciation of life
in my sensitivity to the world
My love for you
is present everywhere because
it is the emotional side of me
that is a part
of everything I do
I love
my love
for you

What a comfort
What a treat
What an absolutely beautiful feeling
to know that you are
always here
ready to receive my love
ready to offer me your love
Never could I ask for anything
more wonderful
than you

When I am feeling elated
or when I am feeling sad
I know that you will understand me
When I want to go off all by myself
or when I want to be with a lot of people
I know that you will understand me
When I am very quiet
or when I am very talkative
I know that you will understand me
When I do things that do not make sense
or when I appear to be heading
    in the wrong direction
I know that you will understand me
People are very complex
with many different moods
and many different emotions
and many different reasons
for acting the way they do
If we can find
someone to understand and accept
everything we do and feel
it gives us a strength
and confidence
that we could not get
alone
Thank you for being
the person who
so sensitively
understands me

Sometimes it is hard
to put feelings into words
but I want you to know
how you affect me
When I wake up
and see you in the morning
I am so happy
that we are together
that we are sharing
our lives with one another
I respect you
I admire you
I love you deeply
When I wake up
each morning
and see you next to me
no matter what happens
I know that my
day will
be
all right

Life has no meaning
without you
You are such an important
part of me
that alone
I am not whole
I know that this is not
a popular thing to say
but I am proud of it
because our relationship is
so total and
so encompassing and
so fulfilling
We have blended our
souls, hearts and minds into
one person
who is always understood and loved
and who can never be lonely
except when apart
I love you

I am a confident and
self-sufficient person, but,
yes, I am much more happy
when Stephen, the person
I love so much, is with me.
SPS

Some of my friends
live on the other side of the country
from me. I rarely see them, but when
something important happens to us,
we immediately call each other,
and it is as if we were
never apart.

—SPS

Though we don't see each other very much
nor do we write to each other very much
nor do we phone each other very much
I always know that, at any time,
I could call, write or see you
and everything would be exactly the same
You would understand everything I am saying
and everything I am thinking

Our friendship does not depend
on being together
It is deeper than that
Our closeness is something inside of us
that is always there
ready to be shared with each other
whenever the need arises

It is such a comfortable and warm feeling
to know that
we have such a lifetime
friendship

Love is an emotion
so complete that it encompasses
your entire being
You feel like
you are a part
of the other person
Love is an excitement
a sharing
a truth
a unity
Love makes your body more alive
your soul more tender
and your life more beautiful
Because of you
I am able to feel
the true
meaning of love

People who criticize art, writing, or
movies that have a stable and happy
theme most often have very unhappy
lives themselves. Since they are miserable,
they are unable to relate to anyone's
ability to enjoy life. And they criticize
all that reflects happiness.
The poem on this page was written
recently and the poem on the next
page was written many years ago—
with the hope of making these
kinds of people less afraid
to love.   SPS

When love is beautiful
the poem about love
should be beautiful
but if it is
there are those people
who call it "light and soppy"

When the sky is clear blue
and the mountain's air crisp
the play about nature
should be beautiful
but if it is
there are those people
who call it "light and soppy"

When the birds sing
and the flowers bloom
the song about life
should be beautiful
but if it is
there are those people
who call it "light and soppy"

But when
love is unrequited
and suicide contemplated
these same people
call the creation a work of art

Something is very wrong
when people are so
ashamed of beautiful feelings
and they call them "light and soppy"
while being so proud of anguish
that they equate it
with being an intellectual
They will never be
free from themselves
to experience any kind
of beauty in their lives

If people were less afraid to love
perhaps there would be less hatred
in the world

The one thing I am shocked about in my life is how much I love being a mother to my three beautiful children. I never, for one second of my high school, college, or early married years, envisioned myself as a mother. I was a writer, devoting my time and energy to my career and to my love, Stephen. Now the most important part of my life is my family. Everything else comes after that.

SPS

I am always here
to understand you
I am always here
to laugh with you
I am always here
to cry with you
I am always here
to talk to you
I am always here
to think with you
I am always here
to plan with you
Even though we
might not always
be together
please know that
I am always
here to
love
you

You are a
woman to
be honored
a woman who
knows what she wants to do
and will do it
a woman who
is not afraid to
speak out for what she believes
a woman who
is kind and good and giving
yet wants for herself also
a woman who
sets high goals for herself
and achieves them
a woman who
is beautiful on the outside
and inside
a woman who
understands her body and
is in complete charge of her body
a woman who
is a success at work
and with those she loves
a woman who
is intelligent and sensitive
strong and able
a woman
who loves being
a woman
equal to men
a woman
who is
the ideal
woman

Y ou are a remarkable woman
accomplishing so much as a strong woman
in a man's world
strong but soft
strong but caring
strong but compassionate

You are a remarkable woman
accomplishing so much as a giving woman
in a selfish world
giving to your friends
giving to your family
giving to everyone

You are a remarkable woman
who is loved by so many people
whose lives you have touched
including mine

This poem was written to my doctor
and friend, the late Katherine Carson,
who so ably delivered two of my
children. She was the most dedicated
doctor I have ever met, devoting
eighteen hours every day to making
women healthy, while also fighting
for the equality of women.
        Actually, there are no words
strong enough or beautiful
enough to describe
        my friend.
            SPS

I want to get
to know you better
What do you like to do
in your spare time
What do you think about
when you are not working
Do you like to walk
in the woods in solitude
Do you like politics and
what is going on in the world today
What kind of people do you like
What are your moods like
What do you think
a man's and woman's role should be
Let's get together
I want to get
to know you better

I spent a lot of time
meeting all kinds of people
I had a lot of fun
and learned a lot
Though each person I met
had great characteristics
something was missing
No one person
had all the qualities that
I had hoped a person could have:
someone whose every action
    and thought I could respect
someone who was very intelligent
    yet could also be fun-loving
someone who was sensitive, yet virile
exciting and sensuous
someone who knew what they wanted out of life
a beautiful person inside and out
I could not find a person like this
until I met you

Since I had so many
requirements for the person
I would love, no one ever
measured up to my dreams
until I met
Stephen.

SPS

So many times each day
I am reminded of you
I do things that we did together
I hear things that we heard together
I see things that we saw together
So many times each day
I am reminded of you
And at the end of every day
I think of the memories
and I just want to say
thanks

I went to a college campus and immediately thought of my college roommate and all the things we did together. I saw people who looked like us. I listened to conversations that sounded like us. I had a wonderful time reminiscing about our college days.

SPS

When things happen fast
I think about you
When things are slow
I think about you
When the sun shines
or the rain pours down
I think about you
When the clouds become thunderous
or the rainbow appears at the end of the sky
I think about you
I guess I think about you
all the time
because everything I see
that is beautiful
reminds me of you

Stephen needed to go away for a day. I took a walk, and everything I thought about included him. Stephen is such an important part of my life that when we are apart, I feel as if he is right next to me.
SPS

When things are confused
I discuss them with you
until they make sense

When something good happens
you are the first person I tell
so I can share my happiness

When I don't know what to do in a situation
I ask your opinion
and weigh it heavily with mine

When I am lonely
I call you
because I never feel alone with you

When I have a problem
I ask for your help
because your wiseness helps me to solve it

When I want to have fun
I want to be with you
because we have such a great time together

When I want to talk to someone
I always talk to you
because you understand me

When I want the truth about something
I call you
because you are so honest

It is so essential
to have you in my life
Thank you for being my love

Love is
    being happy for the other person
        when they are happy
    being sad for the person
        when they are sad
    being together in good times
    and being together in bad times
Love is the source of strength

Love is
    being honest with yourself at all times
    being honest with the other person at all times
    telling, listening, respecting the truth
    and never pretending
Love is the source of reality

Love is
    an understanding so complete that
    you feel as if you are a part of the other person
    accepting the other person just the way they are
    and not trying to change them to be something else
Love is the source of unity

Love is
    the freedom to pursue your own desires
    while sharing your experiences with the other person
    the growth of one individual alongside of
    and together with the growth of another individual
Love is the source of success

Love is
   the excitement of planning things together
   the excitement of doing things together
Love is the source of the future

Love is
   the fury of the storm
   the calm in the rainbow
Love is the source of passion

Love is
   giving and taking in a daily situation
   being patient with each other's needs and desires
Love is the source of sharing

Love is
   knowing that the other person
   will always be with you regardless of what happens
   missing the other person when they are away
   but remaining near in heart at all times
Love is the source of security

Love is
   the
source
   of
life

I tried to define love, but it is impossible to capture the essence of love in words. For Love, to me, is far deeper and greater than any words can explain.
SPS

If you know what you believe in
and if you stick to these beliefs,
Life will be easier because you
will have a clear-cut
path to follow.
SPS

I Believe in You

I believe in knowing oneself
and what one can do and wants to do in life
I believe in setting goals
and working hard to achieve them
I believe in having fun
every day in every way
I believe in creativity
as an expression of one's feelings
I believe in sensitivity
in viewing the world
I believe in the family
as a stable and rewarding way of life
I believe in love
as the most complete and
    important emotion possible
I believe in you
as a necessary part of my life
I believe in you
and love you
forever

Someone asked me what
age I liked best
She told me that she
liked best the past days
in high school
I felt bad for her
because it meant that
she is not as happy now
as she was in the past
I know I liked my life
during my school days
but I like my life
even better now
And the reason is
simple —
I am freer
I am more content
I am excited about every aspect of life
but most of all
I like my life better now because
I have you
in my life now

I think it is very important
to live life to its fullest. Love.
Have fun. Work. Relax. Achieve.
Do a lot of interesting things.
Make each day better than the
previous day so that you won't look
back to the "old days" as the best.
The best day should be today.

SPS

We have formed
a friendship
that has become
invaluable to me
We discuss our goals
and plan our future
We express our fears
and talk about our dreams
We can be very serious
or we can just have fun
We understand each other's lives
and try to encourage each other
in all that we do
We have formed
a friendship
that makes our lives
so much
nicer

I feel sort of empty when Stephen is
not with me. I feel an urge to show
him each pretty tree that I see
or discuss an idea that I have.
I get by during the day, but the
day would be so much more
complete if Stephen were
there to share it
with me.
SPB

When you are not here
I do everything I am supposed to do
trying to act normal and happy
when all of a sudden
I see something that reminds
me of you
and I sadly realize
how far away
you really are
For a few minutes I stop
everything I am doing and
I think about one of our
beautiful memories
This brings a real
smile to my face
and helps me to
get through the day
But it sure would
be nicer
if you were here with
me
I miss you
so much

ABOUT THE AUTHORS

Susan Polis Schutz began writing at age seven, and to the delight of millions of readers, she has been writing ever since. She is the author of seven best-selling books of poetry—Come Into the Mountains, Dear Friend; I Want to Laugh, I Want to Cry; Peace Flows from the Sky; Someone Else to Love; Yours If You Ask; Love, Live and Share; and Find Happiness in Everything You Do.

Susan grew up in a small country town, Peekskill, New York. She graduated from Rider College earning degrees in English and biology. After attending graduate school, majoring in physiology, in New York City, Susan taught elementary school and wrote articles for magazines and newspapers.

In 1965 she met Stephen Schutz. Stephen, a native New Yorker, studied at the New York High School of Music and Art where he practiced the basics of drawing and calligraphy. His great love and appreciation of art became overshadowed by physics books and lab tables at M.I.T. and Princeton University (where he received a Ph.D. degree in theoretical physics in 1970), but it surfaced again when he moved to Colorado for post-graduate work.

Following his marriage to Susan in 1969 and his increasing love for his inspirational surroundings, Stephen decided to give up his career in physics. This decision allowed him to devote his time to the development and perfection of his artistic techniques, and it gave Stephen and Susan the opportunity to do what they most wanted to do . . . spend their time together.

In 1972 Come Into the Mountains, Dear Friend, Susan's first book of poems with Stephen's illustrations, was published. The public acceptance of this book was phenomenal, and history was made in the process. It became apparent that people readily identified with Susan's poetic words and Stephen's mystical illustrations, and by the end of that year, their joint career, combined with a very special love, became their way of life.

Susan and Stephen pursue creative paths which continually diverge and meet again. A variety of interests and concerns keeps them involved in new and exciting things. In addition to designing and illustrating all of Susan's books, Stephen Schutz has artistically complemented the works of many other well-known authors. He has also created beautiful notecards, calendars and prints featuring his gentle airbrush blends, beautiful oil paintings, unique calligraphy and exceptional photography. A man of many interests, Stephen continues to study physics as a hobby and maintains his special rapport with the outdoors, manifested in his frequent hiking trips in the mountains, swimming in the ocean and cross-country skiing along the Continental Divide. Stephen is truly a very talented and "self-contained" man.

In addition to Susan's books of poetry, many of her poems have been published on notecards and prints and in national and international magazines and textbooks. She has also edited books by other well-known authors. Susan has also coauthored a woman's health book entitled **Take Charge of Your Body**. Susan is currently writing an autobiographical novel. The conviction with which Susan expresses feminist ideas does not preclude an equally intense commitment to her family. Her efforts to weave together a modem female independence with the classical idea of love is a source of harmony in her work.

A special kind of talent is required to translate feelings into poems and emotions into paintings, and Susan and Stephen have that rare gift. It is a gift that has been shared with more than 300 million people around the world. Susan and Stephen's works have been translated into Spanish, German, Hebrew, Finnish, Arabic, Dutch, Afrikaans and Japanese, and have been published in the rest of the nations of the world. In a time of constant fluctuation in social, religious and political standards, Susan and Stephen's expressions serve to remind us all of our inner spirit and our basic values. As a British newspaper recently commented, "Her modern freestyle poems, matched by his artistry, touch the soul."

Photo by Barry Staver

Photo by Barry Staver